Colour to Save the Ocean
Book One

A Colouring Book for Children

Illustrated by Kasia Niemczynska
Text by Karin Holloway

My Fat Fox Ltd
MMXIV

My Fat Fox Ltd
86 Gladys Dimson House
London E7 9DF
United Kingdom
www.myfatfox.co.uk

Colour to Save the Ocean – Book One
© 2014 Kasia Niemczynska

http://nkassia.com/

Cover design © 2014 Kasia Niemczynska and Paul Holloway

ISBN 978-1-905747-41-2

For Mum and Greg

"Only a life lived for others is a life worthwhile."

A. Einstein.

About the artist

Kasia is a London based illustrator. With her trusted pilot pen, graphite and immense collection of colour markers she creates quirky and colourful images. She mostly focuses on portraying people and animals, carefully bringing out all the important, detailed features and then adding her own colourful twist to them. "Animals are one of my favourite themes. I think they are the best models! It gave me lots of joy to be part of the My Fat Fox project to help conservation groups to Save the Ocean. There's nothing more rewarding than using your skills and contributing them to something really special".

Contents

Atlantic Spadefish 7

Clown Fish 11

Coral Reef 15

Crab 19

Dolphins 23

Flying Fish 27

Jellyfish 31

Lobster 35

Moorish Idol 39

Octopus 43

Orcas 47

Penguins 51

Atlantic Spadefish

Young Spadefish stay near the shore
to hide by looking like leaves.

Clown Fish

Beautiful Clownfish are yellow, orange, and red with white and black lines.

Coral Reef

A coral reef is a colourful Ocean garden and many different kinds of animals live there.

Crab

Crabs and corals come in all sizes and beautiful colours and live on the reef.

Dolphins

Dolphins swim up and down with their families, talking to each other, and sometimes swim with people.

Flying Fish

Flying Fish swim very fast and torpedo themselves out of the water to use their big fins to fly before returning to the Ocean.

Jellyfish

You can see through jellyfish and they come in many beautiful light colours but they can sting!

Lobster

Lobster parents hold hands with their
child as they walk together.

Moorish Idol

Moorish Idols live on reefs and are yellow, black and white with a very long white fin on top.

Octopus

An octopus can hide on the Ocean floor by changing how it looks or it can swim very fast to get away.

Orcas

Orca Whales swim close to ice with their heads out of the water to look for food.

Penguins

Penguins live on islands to raise their children and they slide on the ice to dive into the Ocean.

www.ingramcontent.com/pod-product-compliance
Lightning Source LLC
Chambersburg PA
CBHW081422270326
41931CB00015B/3378